THE ORCHARD HOUSE

THE ORCHARD HOUSE

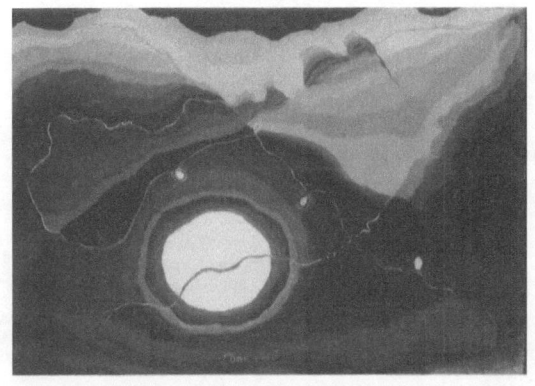

Poems by

Richard Shaw

Antrim House
Bloomfield, Connecticut

Copyright © 2019 by Richard Carlyle Shaw

Except for short selections reprinted for purposes of
book review, all reproduction rights are reserved.
Requests for permission to replicate should
be addressed to the publisher.

Library of Congress Control Number: 2019930280

ISBN: 978-1-943826-54-4

First Edition, 2019

Printed & bound by Ingram Content Group

Book design by Rennie McQuilkin

Front cover painting by Arthur Dove: "Me and the Moon, 1937"
courtesy of The Bridgeman Art Library
and The Phillips Collection

Author photograph by Stephanie Craig

Antrim House
860.217.0023
AntrimHouseBooks@gmail.com
www.AntrimHouseBooks.com
400 Seabury Dr., #5196, Bloomfield, CT 06002

for my parents,
Richard and Elizabeth

Acknowledgments

Grateful acknowledgment to the editors of the following publications in which these poems first appeared, at times in earlier versions:

Blue Lyra Review: "Night Music"
Eunoia Review: "Lumen," "Openings into Things"
The Galway Review: "September," "Three Summer Openings," "Residence in the Rain," "The Second Anniversary of my Father's Death," "Beginning of October"
Hummingbird: sections of "May Rain"

Thanks

To Hillel Krauss who has read closely and listened deeply, helping me hold this body of work as it took form. To the invaluable close reading and listening of fellow poets Wally Swist, Katherine Parker and Bronwyn Louw. To Rennie McQuilkin at Antrim House for the great enthusiasm he has shown and the insight he has brought to this project. To the encouragement of important early teachers: Marshall Hunt, Jack Moore and poets William Zander and Stephen Sandy. And finally, to Astrid, for bringing such grace.

Table of Contents

Dawnings / 1
Evening Bell / 2
September / 3
Openings into Things / 5
Floating World / 9
Lumen / 11
End of Summer / 12
Nomads / 13
Flurry / 15
Beginning of October / 16
Tropic of Capricorn / 17
Winter Midnight / 18
Solstice / 19
Firmament / 20
Night Music / 21
Scarlet Tanager / 23
On the Second Anniversary of My Father's Death / 26
May Rain / 28
Susurrous / 29
Rose / 30
Residence of the Rain / 31
Three Summer Openings / 33
Midsummer / 34
Evensong / 35
Loose Thread / 36
Harbinger / 37
August Stars / 38
Her Overture / 42
Her Song / 45
Horse Mountain / 46
Fathoms of July / 47
Jennings Pond / 49
Mirror / 50

Earth Waiting / 51
Leaning into the Current / 55
Only to Touch / 56
River Epistles / 57
Absence / 59
Two / 60
Ode to Failure / 61
Mutable / 63
Loom / 64
Waking in a Field on an Early Morning in June / 65
Whiff / 66
Fear of God / 67
Vessel / 68
Prelude / 69
Gateway into March / 70
The Neglected / 71
Entreaty to Psyche / 72
Ascending into Night Sky / 73

About the Author / 77
About the Book / 78

*... all my boundaries are in a hurry,
rush out from me and are already elsewhere.*

−Rainer Maria Rilke (from "Narcissus II")

The Orchard House

Dawnings

This golden light
just now unfurling itself
down the face of the western hills
after a long night of arctic air
unwinters something in me

beauty's quiet urgency
shouldering in
jostling
for position

an old *pas de deux*—
our beseeching the world
through astonishment
it unveiling and veiling
around us

freshening now
as it composes itself
towards dawn
       velvet pillow
carrying the crown
of the Queen

Evening Bell

The sky is a cupped dome
reverberations ripple
out from the hills in waves
drifting vessels under sail
holds filled
with bales of dusk

cerulean shimmer
progressing to ultramarine
deepening
through astronomical twilight
to pure umbra
of nightfall

descending darkness
tricks perception
with horizons gone
we float against the sky
the emerald
a jeweler holds up

in that moment
we become
refracted light beam
the fabled green ray
of evening

September

Through the gardens
and out across the fields
everything has passed its fullness
the pokeweed is withering
and the sunflowers'
already poor posture
has worsened

crabapples plink
the porch boards
like a marimba all night
now even my old joys
are worn to a luster
as they come back to find me

~

there's a granite capstone
on an old abandoned well
that when slid off
throws deep reverberations
of low notes
through a woodwind reed
hidden long inside me

in the silence that follows
which lasts for days
are petals just opening

of a blood red flower
I didn't know I contained

~

now at dusk
my hand brushes
against a pile of keys
and through touch alone
fingertips find the one

which unlocks
a grand door
to a ruined cathedral
shimmering with
light-laced

shadows of wings

Openings Into Things

1.

Leaves surge to various reds
begin releasing from the trees
the vividness remaining
is not what most captivates
this autumn
but the bare hollow places
which have opened in between

shadowy tunnels
for our yearning
to leap through

into what?

dawn-lit
forest glades
where antlered creatures
with shining fur
bound between
      shadows
and light

2.

Spiral funnels off oar tips
spun into still surfaces of lakes
swirling portals
offering glimpses

down
through glimmering
viridescence
to mysterious shapes
the stillness of bells
at lake bottom

3.

Microscope
lenses
springing open
galaxies
within
water droplets

or Andromeda's
whorl
deep blue
in Hubble's
unblinking eye

first eyelid opened
of a newborn
letting through
soft pearled
light

from another world

4.

Hole-in-the-ice
eye sockets

of fox skull
found

first summer of
sleep-away camp

delicately chambered
inner chapel
translucent to light

it was less death
 than rapture

my first catch
of breath

5.

Take a good look
 at World
concocting openings
through to herself

holding one end
of a golden string
coaxing our search into

all thought missing

longing
to be found

old key
tucked in a drawer
flying through
        darkness
towards us

already aglow
        at the edges
as it begins
encountering
        the light

Floating World

The red of new buds
bleeds through the fog
then fades
bleeds through
and fades
up this wet path

amorphousness
out of which
shapes emerge
become tree trunks
trail markers
moss covered stones

peals of birdsong
echo through
draped woods
on tips of spruce needles
droplets build
and release

a thrumming
of wingbeats
sweeps overhead
as silent blackbirds pass
flying by feel
with reflections in their eyes

at the summit
the woods open
and fog begins to lift

swirling mists
rinse the air
a polished silver

I squint in the brightness
and am a young boy again
holding my mother's hand
fingering her diamond ring
transfixed by its prism
in the noon sun's glare

Lumen

To walk together
in the solar
flare of the beloved
carrying luminous heart

our ribcages
glass lighthouse beacons
barely containing their little suns

I recall my surprise on
Ocracoke Island at
the discovery of
what a diminutive bulb
a lighthouse actually
contains
        its brilliant beam
all mirror and lens

one enormous reflector
like the one we sometimes feel
at the back of the chest
behind the heart
a dazzling golden amphitheater
catching and magnifying
such radiance
from all that shines

End of Summer

After days of rain
this morning's sky
breaks clear
and September
brings out
her crystal water glasses

mornings
grass is wet with dew
and the water in the lake
is bracing

midday air hums
summer's knot slackens

deep lens of the sky
unfocuses
and in its shimmering
      an image
of a beloved ghost
departing

Nomads

Perched in an oak at 4am
watching the Orionids
meteor shower
light up the sky

phosphorescent sparks
arc across the heavens
flaming arrows released
towards walled fortresses
under siege
      their message
surrender!

keeping quiet vigil
the folds of my brain relax
give up their puzzlement
spread out
empty themselves

like farm landscapes
seen from a plane at night
occasionally
a solitary light will flicker
      someone's awake
down there

in stillness
wedged against
this knotty trunk
the only perceptible sound
ocean-thrum of my blood

sibling to
these cosmic ores
pulsing through space
igniting white hot
as they blaze in the
silk of our atmosphere

I think of all the friends in my life
those who are here
those no longer here
and whisper to each one . . .

Come in
under the canopy
of these glowing sparks
and let us spend this brief time
that we have . . .

together

Flurry

Counting the friends in my life
first snowflakes of December
are they many? are they few?

Beginning of October

Whisperings over the field
the faithful among the goldenrod
returning gifts of summer
bow like mourners
to a lament
sung by katydids

Tropic of Capricorn

Out in the early darkness
standing on the soft
turned earth
of last season's garden

my breath cloud
makes constellations
gleam

Winter Midnight

Cassiopeia
slows overhead
sparkling like crystal
        chandelier

ancient sentinel
over our lives in the dark
pinwheeling northwards
your hem trails our sleep

~

Shattering through
snow glaze
at the hilltop
I press upwards in starlight
reaching to stroke
        her bare foot

so intimate and close is she now
in the January night

Solstice

Longest night of the year
all appearances
indicate an ending
semblance of death

though in fact
a beginning
new warmth
uncurling
in the seed's germ

almost imperceptible
is night's
subtle turning
from deep indigo
to nascent rose

all is emergent
as we lift our faces to meet
fledgling light
on this foremost
of mornings

with such confidence
sun's pale ray
now brimming the horizon
      crimsons
closed eyelids

Firmament

Los Cerrillos, NM

Kneeling on parched earth
sharing this patch of high desert
with scattered bunches of
yellow wildflowers which
smell of lemon when crushed

I've memorized a single
flower's pattern
star cluster from deepest space
in order to look it up later and
discover its name

majestic cloud formations plume
slowly transforming
their architecture in silence
their distant magenta shadows
move like veils across the desert floor

the stillness around me
is a quilt made of air
each passing moment weightless
and bell-like the gentle swaying
of one into the next

Night Music

for Mstislav Rostropovich (1927-2009)

1.

My house tonight
is a bathysphere
on a deep sea expedition
down into the Bach Cello Suites

we plunge steadily
as surface light disappears
and the pressures build
our small porthole beams light
that can be seen from the ocean floor

2.

The No. 4 Suite has just begun
the high-wire act of its opening bars
they whirl unfettered
notes cascading loose-limbed
in perfect harmonic progression
hovering over an invisible net

it's the maestro's late recording
the one where he's holding
as much loss between his arms
as cello

3.

The ocean floor ripples
from the vibrating strings
barnacled ribs
of old shipwrecks hum
as the slow sarabande
echoes through the deep

through emerald sea light
eyes open since the Pleistocene
a giant manta ray sails
coursing through whorls of sound
while synchronizing the slow riffling
of its great wings

4.

These deep sea contemplations
transform each time they are played
even in my small sanctuary
in the middle of the night
with the candles guttering
and the pines shushing like waves

an old gnarled hand
nimbly balancing a bow
pleads out chords
the way an oyster meticulously
buffs a rough grain of sand
into the opal of rising moon

Scarlet Tanager

At a bend in the path
sudden streak of red
beats through the woods
flits over marsh

vibrancy of air
I speak your name aloud
mouthful of rhythm
retrieved from childhood

words my mother conferred
when language
was sparkling new
and each noun shone

backyard meadow run
brook-bound
through timothy
to the shakuhachi flute
of your call

you dove for gnats
above still pools
minnow-shimmering
in summer heat

now you have returned
incandescent
flaring across
the pond this morning

       Orphean
your name is song
      you move between worlds

convey the bygone
into presence

~

    in my case
it was an old shoebox
hidden at age six
in the dark root caverns
of a giant oak

treasure chest
lined in odd scraps of silk
bearing
prized marbles
picture cards
    a small wooden flute
in the shape of a bird

bounty
announcing my young self
and childhood's
    incorruptible
eternal

bright companion
ever most deep
the deepest reds

of your breast
    so sorrowful

it is beyond measure
all that we leave behind

On the Second Anniversary of my Father's Death

Rising early
heading to the hilltop
to be alone with you
now that you've become
the early light

eastern sky
uncloaks in layers
steadily
overtaking night

skiffs of cirrus
assemble
above the horizon
hulls reddening

birds pipe
new bright notes
as dawn materializes
out of nothing

spiced scents
of black-eyed Susans
intensify memory

it's the simplest things
you showed me
I am finally
able to learn

arriving late
like this light
with all it knows

May Rain

sparrow twitter
like chiming bells
rings out from under

apple blossoms
in the rain

~

daybreak ignites
a dark ceiling
of clouds

the lilac
throws its
blue shadow

~

birch trees
vanish
under frills of mist

like shy girls
at a party

Susurrous

A surprise of rain
arrives at daybreak
sluicing off eaves
in silver rills

an incantatory
ping pinging
gently lifts me
from sleep

in the dream
I was splashing
through a brook's swift
with a girl
whispering songs
in a lisp

Rose

Spring's
green flame
parts
lips

then
its tongue
delectably
licks

Residence in the Rain

Sitting on the shore
of Fitzgerald Lake
height of the lavender
water lily bloom
just as it begins to rain

the sound
rising from silence
builds
to an all-encompassing
gamelan

torrent's
soft mallets
play lily pads
striking flower-petal
xylophones

rain refuses
our being separate
denies us autonomy
draws us in
to become part of its story

passing through
silver veils
we enter stillness
of canyons
inside of the rain

astonished
to discover
in most ephemeral
of dwellings
such boundless shelter

Three Summer Openings

A stream's
water flute
calls over rocks
but after
     look
dawn's vermilion gate

~

Wild turkeys single file
a noontide orchard
heads bobbing
above the clover
like swimmers in a river

follow that fresh trail
to an entry in the hemlocks
push through boughs of
deep shade
into timelessness

~

July heat wave
tiger lilies in bloom

tiny lanterns of fireflies
light the meadow at dusk

Midsummer

To savor these days
delighting in the heat
to cherish these small scratches
that sting on my arms

gathering wet
tiger lilies this afternoon
by the river
wrestling them

all the way home
and into this too small vase
where they reassemble
in arias of deep ochre

Evensong

Longest evening
of summer
singsong
refrains
from children's
hiding games
echo
through the streets
at dusk

Loose Thread

Carefree
summer day
from my
      childhood

I relive you

Harbinger

A single cloud shadow
shaped like a pool toy
sea serpent

just giddy-upped
across the scrim
of morning hills

and August begins

August Stars

*The most beautiful order in the world
is found in the random gatherings of things.*
         – Heraclitus

Queen Anne's lace is
bursting in the orchard
a sweeping river of
star constellations
waist-high under the apple trees

flowers sway and part
as I pass among them
their broad heads—
upraised palms
carrying the bier
of this late August sky

~

It's been a season of
Beethoven piano sonatas
steep wooded hikes
and Heraclitus on the *Fire of Being*
of long light-filled days
and deep nights tracking
Hercules across the sky

these late sonatas
move like weather
through inner atmosphere

their ascending lines
are thermal updrafts
rendering bright cumulus heights

their startling plunges
a maelstrom
rolling through treetops
by storm light

a harmony of opposites
pressed against the
imperturbable
heart of summer

~

In a dream at the solstice
I saw my bones
lying in the grass
and apart further still
my jawbone unattached

awoke
silver morning
with the words . . .
my beautiful skeleton
trailing in midair

wondered
will there be lightness
as I lift from my body some day

husk falling back on the earth
shed tenderly away

~

Whether embraced by
these piano movements
or bending to take in
the honey scent
of Queen Anne's lace
autumn's mirror flashes
in late summer air

it slips out of concealment briefly
then recedes
leaving a momentary coolness
a catch in the chest

the expansiveness
of summer
       pulling free

a tide going out

~

Now the final sonata's themes
are clarifying
reaching their coda

resolving towards a final chord
which itself refines

to a single note
        hovering there
a struck bell
a glistening pearl
the evening star
        —white anemone

just now visible
over the western ridge

an annunciation
electric
through twilit air

Her Overture

1.

Horse Mountain is a woman
she takes on forms
casts them off at will
season after season
in the passageways
of the earth
and through the air above
she has bees
strides between worlds
is a stream

2.

A doe in the fir woods
discovers her voice
first morning of spring
turns to a woman
at wood's edge
and without breaking step
slips sylphlike
into newly green
dew-wet bracken

      trembling
such is her joy
exalting freshness of language
she moves into the field

conferring names
pronouncing word
after word
of praise

3.

At midday
soaring on updrafts
I watch a red tailed hawk
transfigure into woman
her wingspan flashing
as tip feathers catch silver
off cumulonimbus
smooth skin of her breast
now deepening to crimson
as she banks into cloud shadow
gliding watchfully
alert
no Icarus—
she aspires to earth
      and tucking
magnificently
dives

4.

Reclining she is hillside
her thoughts move
in the undergrowth
her utterance
a clear spring

issuing from the earth
susurrant through cress
murmurous over rocks

settling in deep stillness
her voice comes clear
modulating above
stream sound
underwater
as in the air
her presence
        unbound

I recognize you
heard you in the trees
watched you by the stream
felt you near at moonrise

so regarded
she surges in attendance
sings through water
rapturous
at being seen

Her Song

All the excited particles
make up the daylight
for you

the skies in summer
reach endlessly
for you

as their blue fades
at dusk
and the brilliant stars appear

the rondo of the Milky Way
for you
shall always
be a shelter

Horse Mountain

Sumptuous June night
doors and windows open
drawing blossom fragrant air
reading by lamplight
moths and junebugs
patter the screens

at dawn
I wake to meet the gaze
of a large stag
standing in the orchard
we study each other
eye to eye
        a full minute
before he slowly ambles away

I make tea
go to my bookcase
pick out favorite poems

all day I am a released arrow

at dusk
        fireflies
and by nightfall
watery trill
of a wood thrush

my small orchard house
is a ship launched at night
which sails out under stars
to moor again at first light

Fathoms of July

Days are hot and muggy
heatwave
is how we speak of it
arms stick to table tops
glasses sweat
clothing must be peeled off
and the sun shows its serious side

but the nights . . .
nights are silken and feral
ringing bell choirs
of katydids carol
over bass flutes of owls

in the luxurious dark
night's vehicle rolls out beyond
the far edges of the land
high up over buildings
and the canopies of trees

there the summer night
assembles its orchestra
while a parchment colored moon
runs its beam
over quiet houses

where falling asleep
in the warm darkness
is being tossed in the sea at night
floating in the swell
just beyond the break

dark shapes which startle
at the edge of sight
soon become familiar
as we recognize them
sinking down
into the very first dream

Jennings Pond

for Leslie

Light washes you
sitting
arm lengths away
the braids
rushing down the hillside
of your back
are like those twin streams
in the North Bennington woods
I would take in two leaps

morning flushed at the window
and the right side of the face
I was beginning to know
shone
the color of early spring

after you left
I walked down to the pond's edge
and the water became
the other side of your face
the side in shadow
the side the reeds bend towards

I listened as your stillness
became the cricket sound
and watched a flock of birds
lifting above the trees
make the same small gesture
you do when you find me
with your eyes

Mirror

Standing in front of Vermeer's
Girl With a Pearl Earring
on loan to The Frick Collection
in New York

last time near her
was twenty years before
at the Mauritshuis
in The Hague

it's remarkable
how much
she's changed
these intervening years

back then
she was innocent
lighthearted
and alluring

now
her face reveals
unexpected
depths

and a sadness
behind the eyes
which captures a quietness
within me

such a deep spring
this knowledge
she came by

Earth Waiting

I terra non firma

Through moonlit darkness
I could see across the yard
to a deeper darkness
at the wood's edge
saw my death there
waiting for me

felt death
dear companion
not beckoning
just quietly waiting
unhurried
in the threshold of the pines

slipping downhill
a night mist curled
settling in pear trees
in wait
to accommodate
my future transparency

zeroing the scales
earth fathomed me
conveying weight
down root tangles
through hushed rooms
arranged for my bones

at night's balance point
eastern sky

shedding darkness
the indisputable proposal
of my death
waited for me in the earth

II *coronation*

Brushing aside coneflowers
in the predawn dark
an invitation
as ground opens ahead
descending stair
to warmly lit chamber

at its center a bed
with quilt of star moss
embroidered
in purple phlox
fine lace of old leaves

a grand headboard
luminous gold
displaying vignettes
a history of the world
all interwoven storyline

in a corner of this tableau
single thread glow
brighter than the rest
revealing this life's arc
poised mid-gesture

ascend now
to meadow-sweetened air
lifting to morning dewfall
mantle of daybreak
resting lightly

center of an orchard
mounting out of earth's sleep
this bright trace
a bestowal
      fleeting
as breath on glass

Leaning Into the Current

Hearing for the first time
at seventeen that stunning
ground-giving-way free fall
of the first bars of the Bach
Cello Suite No. 2 in D minor
and realizing... *My God,
there is profound sadness in life...
and I haven't experienced it yet.*

Only To Touch

Green scarf snagged
waving
beneath the ice

knelt to chip through
with skate blade strike
after strike

only to obscure
by opaque white
what had been limpid clear

stopped before
what once dazzled
altogether disappeared

River Epistles

shoulders of
river stones
muscled smooth
down centuries

~

rapids clack
stone against
stone burnishing
the shallows

~

deep water
bends light
worlds beneath
the surface

~

a clear
pool leaves
backflip and
disappear under

~

receding water
flotsam left

here there
storms' surge

~

river's history
recorded in
bottom sand
over lifetimes

Absence

settles us in the heart
heart expands in longing

as it does through love
though with longing

estuary tides reverse
draw back up the rivers

flood the lowlands
reach far

trailing moonlight
over the dense

flowering water lilies
of remembrance

Two

Waking
unbridles the heart

as it rears
clutch it's wild mane
then lean into
a gallop

race with me

~

I dreamt
we walked for hours
through the snow
together

spoke
of new journeys
      and laughed
watching each other's breath
frost into clouds

Ode to Failure

*... how necessary a World of Pains
and troubles is to school an Intelligence
and make it a soul.*
– John Keats

Of all the great sorrows
a coming-up-short of life

let me know
this song as well

I've garnered
subtle treasures

lit noon fires
but let me sing of

foundering
and want of triumph

all thin years
the unfulfilled stares

most pale
though occasionally

a blossoming
presses through these

promise takes root
within this *vale of tears*

this lowland
of soul-making

this fragile sun
and rain shower world

Mutable

I've watched
that clear pond
far edge of the meadow
put on its summer sky mask
take it off
swap
for its falling stars mask

observed it
over weeks
shuffling through others
      rippled surface
        mirrored wood's edge
        thunderhead

settling
upon each new guise
capriciously

Loom

I *love* that poem . . .

that poem which
by handling warp and weft
came through me

disentangled me

thank you, thank you

Waking in a Field
on an Early Morning in June

Good morning, body!

Good morning, individuality
       that I call . . . "me"

Whiff

Yellow box truck
parted
sweet-scented
humid air
and in its wake
from the garden
across the road
astringent surprise
of *marigold!*

Fear of God

All it took
was my cracking
open a window
for that chipmunk
on the fence
to point its tail
straight to the sky
then bolt to earth
clothing itself
again
in the garden

Vessel

Two feet of snow
and *three* poems finished

such beneficence
so gracefully placed

in the chipped
upturned bowl

time spent alone
has fashioned me into

Prelude

Austere beauty
of a stubble field
in January

little evidence
of hidden symphonies
rehearsing
underground

Gateway Into March

Through lashing branches
blinding winds
matted dead grass
and winter-strewn jetsam

we pause
in wan half-light
expectant
amidst the tumult

while unfamiliar parts of us
crowd
along the rim of the world
waiting
to be born

The Neglected

Alone in the serene house
books alphabetized on the shelves
the furniture all tastefully arranged
long bands of December sunlight
reach across the floor
and press against the walls

suddenly out of this quiet
a rustling movement of vine growth
erupts upwards out of my center
twines up the back of my throat
flourishes into leaf over my tongue
and bursts forth out of my mouth

wild roots sprout from my legs
breaking through the floorboards
snaking around pipes and wires
cracking the foundation
to branch downwards into the earth

in the stunned silence
I ask, oddly unalarmed . . . *What are you?*
response: *Your feral life.*

Entreaty to Psyche

Weave wondrous dream
unite me with your realm
let me traverse
the ceaseless unspooling
of your visions

when waking tugs
I will ferry us to surface
where you may slip free
into the opulence beneath

nape of my neck
still carrying
the guiding touch of your hand
from the shining dark
where worlds meet

Ascending Into Night Sky

1.

Tonight's clear star watch
footprint calligraphy
up snowbound hill
the snow field glinting
in bright lakes of moonlight

Arcturus flashes
a beacon
signaling Rigel
across half the heavens
in symbols long forgotten

agile Orion pivots
graceful dervish
while the Pleiades bristle
faint but majestic
training their soft light
earthwards

Ptolemy wrote reverently
of these seven maidens
and the Babylonians
on their papyrus charts
called them Star of Stars

winter night sky
river of phosphorescence
infinite points shimmer

mirrored in bright traces
aglow in the brain

fallen from these heights
we drop into ourselves

faces swept
by threads of light

fully formed
if elaborately flawed

       we arrive
             radiant
and appear
to shine

2.

In winter
when nights make up
the better part of our days
the sleeper hovering
up near the ceiling in the dark

slips tethers further
widening into dream
borne through the attic onto the roof
to ascend a ladder up into the sky

where the dreamer
alights off top rungs

into the untamed pink
of a conch shell

which nestles us into its curves
to sail embryonic
over star lanes
a new celestial body
in the sea-spray of planets

3.

As a child
sleepless from fever
drawn from my crib
held in my father's arms
I'm carried to the playroom window
and given my first draft
of vastness—
        pearl of my happiness

I am lifted up
and shown the moon
and higher still
the tail of the Great Bear
as if to say *here* . . .
here is the central gift off your life
to be alive at night
out under the stars

ABOUT THE AUTHOR

Richard Shaw was born in New Jersey and earned his B.A. from Bennington College. He has spent most of his life in the Connecticut River Valley of Massachusetts, where he resides in a venerable New England orchard on Horse Mountain, above Haydenville. A former dancer and choreographer, he maintains a private practice as a Rolfer,° balancing, aligning and making more spacious the human body. *The Orchard House* is his first collection of poems. For more information, please visit www.richardcshaw.com.

This book is set in Garamond Premier Pro, which had its genesis in 1988 when type-designer Robert Slimbach visited the Plantin-Moretus Museum in Antwerp, Belgium, to study its collection of Claude Garamond's metal punches and typefaces. During the mid-fifteen hundreds, Garamond—a Parisian punch-cutter—produced a refined array of book types that combined an unprecedented degree of balance and elegance, for centuries standing as the pinnacle of beauty and practicality in type-founding. Slimbach has created an entirely new interpretation based on Garamond's designs and on compatible italics cut by Robert Granjon, Garamond's contemporary.

Additional copies of this
book can be ordered at all bookstores.

•

Please visit www.AntrimHouseBooks.com
for information on Antrim House books as well as
sample poems, upcoming events, and a "seminar room"
featuring supplemental biography, notes, images, poems, reviews,
and writing suggestions.

www.ingramcontent.com/pod-product-compliance
Lightning Source LLC
Chambersburg PA
CBHW020128130526
44591CB00032B/570